Cup

In *Cup* we meet a poet of rare power and unique originality, unafraid of feeling, able to take on matters of the deepest consequence. Jeredith Merrin strikes me as admirably hard-minded, shunning poeticisms and needless wordage, delivering again and again the real thing. For proof, see the title poem, or the wonderful tribute to John Clare. Plunge in anywhere, and be regaled.
—X.J. Kennedy, judge for the 2013 Able Muse Book Award

Stanzas, rooms, lives./ And you, toiling to make it better,/ whatever your it is./ Each has a cup."

In these forthright and moving poems written in restrained, disciplined stanzas, the stories are told of how we each, "trying to make it better,/ whatever . . . it is," have to find our own cup, and find it acceptable. This is most vividly so in the poems about the bravery and laughter required by a terrible sickness, but also in the very description of a block of still-inhabited Victorian houses, porch after porch, which is like a train going who knows where. The poems' stanzas are the rooms, and in the rooms are the lives.
—David Ferry, winner of the National Book Award

In *Cup,* Jeredith Merrin confronts time's confounding passage, but there's not a glimmer of self-pity here, no mourning the fate of an aging body. Instead she offers us an artful contemplation of what age brings: the strangeness of shifting perspectives, the quiet richness of sustained love, and the unabated force of old griefs. Both witty and meditative, these poems brim with insight and affection. And "Lear's Macaw" alone is worth the price of admission!
—Mark Doty, author of *Paragon Park*

Jeredith Merrin's exhilarating poems pulse with memory, with art, and the complex emotional richness that is the present. Here is the world: Gilgamesh, Arizona's archeology, the desert landscape and its natural history, Eric Rohmer films, Netflix—and also catastrophe unforgotten, or looming. At the book's heart is a sequence of poems of helpless shock and of the courage of her adult daughter's confrontation with cancer: "She's doing it, my grown/ child, with characteristic kindness and/ intelligence. . . ." We recognize not only a mother's love, but also fury in the midst of crisis, and most movingly, her admiration for the beloved child's acceptance. The wished-for reprieve, "our raft saved for now," is, when it comes, "Easeful." These are understated yet passionate poems that ravish with their gallant dignity. Merrin's *Cup* is large and it is full.
  —Gail Mazur, author of *Figures in a Landscape*

Cup

POEMS BY
Jeredith Merrin

ABLE MUSE PRESS

Able Muse Press

www.ablemusepress.com

Printed in the United States of America

Library of Congress Control Number: 2014948755

ISBN 978-1-927409-34-3 (paperback)
ISBN 978-1-927409-33-6 (digital)

Cover design by Alexander Pepple,
    adapted from the image "K1" by Wojtek Wojcik

Book design by Alexander Pepple

Able Muse Press is an imprint of *Able Muse:* A Review of Poetry, Prose & Art—at
    www.ablemuse.com

Able Muse Press
467 Saratoga Avenue #602
San Jose, CA 95129

For Lisa

Acknowledgments

I am grateful to the editors of the following journals where many of these poems originally appeared, sometimes in earlier versions.

Fiddlehead: "Lands You'll Never See," "Lear's Macaw," "Maker's Mark," "A Woman under the Influence."

The Hudson Review: "Foreign Film Series."

Ploughshares: "The Resistant Reader in the Age of Memoir."

Red Rock Review: "Easy Street Sonnet," "Taking It Slow."

Southern Poetry Review: "Untitled."

The Southern Review: "The Art of Living," "New Year," "Stories," "To John Clare."

Virginia Quarterly Review: "The First Days of It," "Not a Prayer," "Suddenly."

The Yale Review: "Late Harvest," "Surfing the *Pororoca*."

Thanks to editors Don Selby and Diane Boller for selecting "The Resistant Reader in the Age of Memoir" and "Late Harvest" for republication in *Poetry Daily*. In earlier versions, and under different titles, this book was a finalist in national contests: The National Poetry Series (in two separate years), the Barrow Street Poetry Book Prize, the May Swenson Award, the Dorset Prize (Tupelo Press).

My thanks to X.J. Kennedy, and also to Alex Pepple for his editorial help and graphics design. For reading the manuscript and suggesting an improved ordering, heartfelt gratitude to Gail Mazur. Some work was completed at the MacDowell Colony, to whom I am indebted for the gift of time. To poet-friends who have given useful feedback and encouragement over the years: you know who you are, and I do hope you know how much you are appreciated. Special thanks to Helen Deutsch and to Elizabeth Brown Lockman for long-lasting friendship and support.

And, above all, my gratitude to Diane Furtney, whose poetry has inspired me, whose criticism has improved my writing, whose rare company has enlarged my life.

Contents

Cup

I

Surfing the *Pororoca*

All this time unremembered, all this time repressed,
the suffering of childhood: the first openness and zest
that met with . . . what? Humiliations, slaps (with the best
of intentions, as our parents told themselves, lest
we grow "too big for our britches," bad). For some, the worst,
all-out beatings, tortures, molestations never guessed
by outsiders, unnoticed or dismissed
by family members who'd been, themselves, oppressed,
and had remained en-mired, immured, inured. The nest
unsafe, yet you had to trust that you were loved, and so suppressed
your self-respecting rage, erased the memories of your past,
which means enacting the hurt on others: you must.

What if it rushed back, painful memory, now?

Annually, in Brazilian autumn, our spring,
where the mouth of the Amazon meets the Atlantic,
it arrives, the *Pororoca,* which is native Tupi for
"big roar." A tall, upriver-rushing wave, or "tidal bore,"
a twelve-foot wall of water with the rumble of a train
that takes up full-grown trees, piranha, spiders, anaconda,
even local houses, jaguar. . . . Swept up: father's
out-of-nowhere jaguar anger, mother's crushing anaconda envy,
spiderweb shame. Uprooted: stupid, stupefying rules,
Forbidden Trees. Seen and known for what they were.
Release of held-back tears for the helpless child who was
yourself, for any child you hurt in turn, for years of blocked vitality.

It's not for amateurs, it's dangerous, you've never felt so free:
from around the world they come to surf this wave.

Dearly Departed

The friends who alter weirdly
when they marry and drive off
overdressed in a pumpkin coach.
The ones who needed you
when they were needy,
then not any more

—and those you used like that.

Those who disappear because
you're not successful
enough, or too successful.

The ones I cared for
only glancingly, preoccupied
with pulling my cart of ambition.

Or my only sister,
who, to exist, has needed
to pretend I don't.

Sent to bed early
in a house of rules,
we lay in one room
watching it go dark
on long June nights—

whispering, listening
until the lucky children outdoors
stopped their playing.
Side-by-side blue beds.

We threw sticks, laughing, for the same
blond dog.

There is no other life.
It costs us dearly.

The Terminator

Not the movie everyone remembers
where suddenly, a blue flash out of nowhere,
out of the future and onto a street in L.A.,
the newborn, full-grown, superman cyborg arrives,
come to prevent a birth that's going to happen
anyway, in the tortuous time-loop plot—

not it, I mean, but the specific term
for (looking down on earth) the shadow line,
a swath or band, diffuse, of half-dark moving
like a sandstorm or a locust swarm,
marking the progression from day to night

(Dancing in the dark, Death's second self),

but twilight here means sunrise over there,
and in the movie the cyborg ends up ending
before discharging the death for which he was sent,
so the plot continues in the sequels,
the way old stars, their stuff, persist in us,

the way a voice persists in someone's mind,
an old-time singer, or our dead mother calling
my name and my sister's name at twilight,
calling the two of us to come to dinner,
her young voice in the fresh half-dark conflicted,
caught between wanting and not wanting us back.

"A Woman under the Influence"

—For Lisa

Gena Rowlands is falling apart in her madras-cloth minidress
in the restored version of the Cassavetes film made two years
after my similar falling apart—

well, not Gena Rowlands, but her character, "Mabel,"
the right, wrong name for this deracinated dreamer,
conjuring as it does an earthy waitress, chirping "Sweetie"

as she pours your second cup.
At first, we feel sympathy for Mabel's husband,
Peter Falk/"Nick"—a manual laborer bumble-blustering

toward his wife's crack-up and hospital commitment.
When six months later she comes home
—drug-scrubbed and guileless, in a white-collared,

red-and-blue, adult-size, first-grade dress—
we see his culpability, the un-harmless bungler deftly
re-ignoring her reality, re-tutoring her in the craziness

that makes this weak and violent man feel strong.
I've left out Nick's assistant-crazy-maker mother,
as well as Mabel's escape hatch of *Swan Lake.*

I've left out the three children, already left out
by their parents' syndromes and colossal self-absorption:
the chubby preschool girl, who learns where not to turn—

not to either, ever; the bespectacled eldest, working
and working at helping his mother; and the middle boy,
all brown-eyed, needy sweetness.

(In my film-after-the-film, he'd become an alcoholic.)
I didn't notice them so much then, in the '70s,
absorbed as I was in my fresh-divorce sorrow:

the children, I mean, my child—then, as now,
anxiously watchful, constantly overworking.
Her grown-up, burnished shoulders, my hazel-eyed girl.

And now, reading what I've written, my good friend remarks:
*Your poem is too easily self-punishing—and it's unfinished,
since you've left out how you changed yourself
and changed what you could see.*

OK. But is it poetry
to mention recording dreams for a decade,
and longer than that spent with paintings,
movies, and psychoanalytic texts?

No way to put lyrically
my forty-year-old child's phone call—her brave fury
at my absence or distraction, for too much of her childhood,
or my spare and careful response: *I'm sorry.*
Thank you for telling me
how I hurt you and why you're angry.
I can listen now.

Words my long-lived mother
(What story did I tell myself?
That fancy writing could win her?)
had died without saying to me.

The Captain's Table

On a ship: older
people, younger adults,
and then the children—
grouped into different sections,
different cabins.

A kind of happy, vacation time.

The ship is boarded by the enemy
and our older group, alone,
is confined. We realize
they mean to kill all passengers.
But this ship runs on gas:

we have an idea; we don't talk.

We block, *surreptitiously*
(the word half-surfaced in sleep!)
all openings with objects
or with our own bodies—
but not the place where gas,
like car exhaust, is entering
the cabin where we
and all the enemy are.

Our captors, or a captor,
catches on, tries
to open a door to get out.
Someone has locked it,
and a woman
(it might be me)
has hidden the key.

Now we're sitting in a circle
in the room, we old ones, singing;

someone lights a match.

Somewhere else, safe now,
are the children.

We blow up

but then we're saved—
sitting at the Captain's table
with linen napkins and cloth.

We are about to eat
and we know that no one
not at our table
can enjoy it (meaning
everything) as we do.

Some young man near me,
the next table, not
from the locked room,
wants to drink
something delicious
that we are drinking, but
he doesn't have the right
kind of cup to pour into.
And he can't drink because
—we're laughing about it—
he won't share our cup.

Cosmic Haiku

Hidden dimensions,
invisible dark matter:
everyone's story.

Stories

—The MacDowell Colony, September 10-14, 2001

How he was an identical twin and how
at twenty-five his brother started eating
more and more and getting fat
so that the mirror image of himself
changed to a fun-house mirror.

How he himself then started eating
less and less and getting thin,
unconsciously insisting that the sum
of their two weights remain the same.

This made us laugh (he told a story well)
and made for questions, as good stories will—

unsettled because he didn't see himself,
or that it was some secret self he saw?
The fat one, was he trying to hide his beauty
the way some women try to do
beneath un-flimsy, costly veils of flesh,
or was he trying to cast a shadow larger
than the one cast by his brilliant twin?
Wasn't this, anyway, a fairly harmless
way to put more distance between themselves
and the nostalgia of one egg,

which seemed to some of us, non-twins
(although of course we'd never say it),
a disturbing, slightly nauseating fate?

Someone asked, instead, the easy question:
Did you have a language of your own?
Yes, until eight: elaborate baby talk,
something mother discouraged and abhorred.

And what about, what about, their mother?
(That's a question I always want to ask.)
And what about the fact just one was gay,
given those so-called studies to determine
if it's environment, or genes, or what?
(I vote for what.) Would gayness be one way
to solve the riddle: how to return *and* to depart?

In the way of good stories, it didn't end there.
Other twin-like units came to mind,
siblings, spouses, lovers, pairs of friends,
ways we tip the scales to keep the balance . . .

* * *

I had something to say about it that morning,
but now it's the next day, and things have changed.

Whoever it is has hijacked passenger planes
and smashed them into buildings,
with thousands working inside.

For hours, shocked silence,
or fragmentary talk.

Wasn't that a story about two brothers—
the story about how murder entered the world,
our blue-egg, one-egg planet?
I borrowed a copy and found it full of puzzles:
Why did God accept the offering
of the shepherd but not the farmer, Cain?
What did the brothers say (it says they talked)
in the field before the younger's blood was spilt?

At dark, the large group gathered in my cabin,
sipping brandy from unmatched coffee cups.
After a while, we began to sing:
songs from different decades, our various childhoods
—Broadway show tunes, Beach Boys, all-girl groups—
loudly, foolishly laughing, for dear life.

* * *

Another day passed, and with it a day-long migraine,
and then in my sleep last night, I died.

I mean (there must be studies that explain this)
I felt my body lift, then slowly sink
as the bright air of consciousness leaked out
(it made a hissing noise),
and then in the dream I was wakened by two friends
who brought me to see a play about a woman
—not myself, but like myself, yet ancient—
a dream imbued with dazzling happiness.
I have no answers for the questions raised.

                    * * *

Chinese boxes of stories within stories;
dying, and even then, more plays and stories.
Everything with its shadow, like Siamese twins.

Is that it, then, is that how murder began,
how (both brothers inside us) it still goes on?
Stories breeding questions, more eggs of stories—
the firstborn wanting to make them stop,
wanting stories to start and end with him . . .

II

The First Days of It

Spring rain, a muffled rattle. Returning
from shock is harder each decade—here, in
the middle of my seventh. But: not me,
the wrong order. She's doing it, my grown

child, with characteristic kindness and
intelligence, mustering surface and
subterranean resources to do
cancer, which means (although she is widely,

deeply loved) *alone.* The PET scan, day-long
surgery, the port installed. More phone calls . . .

* * *

Today I went to get the tax forms we
needed from the federal building, and
the thick, bald, simultaneously smug
and envious low-level bureaucrat

in his stupid no-color cube told me
they didn't have them: he called them (as if
I'd asked for some boutique, Costa Rican
chocolate) *specialty forms.* Fuck him. Fuck

this small-town city. And as for the knee-
jerk advice—*Positivity*—fuck you.

        * * *

I hadn't heard this before, a new tone
—not the violent protestation I
remember from her childhood, when anger
rose with fever to a fearsome pitch as

she raced through any sickness, refusing
the rider, bucking unfamiliar weight.
It awed me, that wild, unmitigated
sense of something *wrong*—which is how this feels:

to hear in your child's voice a terrible,
gentled acceptance of what must be borne.

* * *

Now, her hair. Little flurries to brush off
her clothing, wet clumps after showering,
blocking the drain. Her good husband banters
—*What do you think, a bonnet?*—stalled at the

open bathroom door, copping a look at
the body he adores. It's not until
the next week that the steroids puff her up:
Your cherubic phase, he quips. This treatment's

like aging (O let them grow old!). Taking
each fresh loss lightly, trying not to care.

Plan B

In those first, numb
days when
he'd asked himself what he'd do
without Lisa,
her husband told me wryly
over coffee,
it had comfortingly come
to him:
I would just move to
the mountains, with Lisa.

Because

Because of the cancer she gets poison
because of the poison nausea comes
because of the nausea she can't drink
water because of not enough water

dehydration and fever because of
dehydration and fever a saline
solution and steroids because of the
steroids no hope of sleep because of no

sleep unrelenting exhaustion because
of exhaustion she's fighting depression . . .

Suddenly

Suddenly—no reason—a good weekend!
It feels, says her e-mail, *so good to feel
good.* Always, a gift for celebration
in this child. After the diagnosis,

what would you do, what would withdrawing I?
She opened her house to the many who
phoned, wishing to bring their small gifts. Then, her
blood count still up (ahead, the Neulasta

injections), she planted sunflowers in
the yard: *My plot of happiness,* she said.

Coastal Highway

The almost-grown boy and his not-quite-middle-aged mom on a road trip involving Disneyland and a college-admission interview. It's deep summer before his senior year: he's just done well on his SATs, and she's three months out of surgery, on a two-week chemo break. They're both excited by their release from doggedness. (In fact, they prefer cats.) What music are they playing along the coastal highway, as they take turns behind the wheel? They are aglow with what they know is an already vanishing form of their love: he's begun dating but still adores no woman more. Their mutual teasing is frequent, which of course is sexual, but also not—sexual in that it's not. He's tall and coming into his beauty; she's holding on to hers. OK—something retro and undemanding, I imagine, that they're listening to—maybe Carole King or the Beatles or the soundtrack to that recent movie about a last-chance country songwriter. Good singers, they sing along. The view is ravishing and precipitous. As it travels out the car's open windows, their easy music, the salt air of the Pacific comes in.

Not a Prayer

One that comes to mind
is very old:

Ninsun, mother of the hero,
beseeches the sun-god that Gilgamesh might go
unharmed on his journey to murder
the monster—
that he be watched over by stars. For this,
she selects her best dress,
climbs the stairs to the roof, and burns
sweet-smelling herbs. As it turns

out, Shamash is only one of several
gods in this story: all take bribes and quarrel.
Who, anymore, in need calls out to them?

Her ancient wish and my wish are the same.

The Visit

—Ohio to Arizona

Maybe in some sea-breezed room-of-one's-own,
or when your acne clears up, your debts, your black mood;

if only you were taken up by those personages in power,
if you could lose weight or acquire that luxury car. . . .

What secret preconditions for the true and perfect life?
Imagine my surprise—with conditions far from perfect:

a near-perfect week. For days her nausea lifted,
and although we'd never not listen for

the whisper of recurrence, her prognosis not so dire.
Spring Quarter finally over, I'd graded fast and flown.

Hours talking, teared-up, laughing on a blanket in her yard.
The vast, plush ship gone down, our raft saved for now—

reality re-burnished, shoulders sun-unstrained,
around us wavelets lapping. Easeful. Celadon.

III

Desert Rain

—Chandler, Arizona

Wet morning in the desert.
I was just asking myself why
if I must be old I can't
at least be more *strange*—
vivid, I guess I meant,
of some peculiar utility.

Yesterday's walk: music I love
(never mind the name)
pouring out a condo window.
Like that, I think I mean:
singular, and unexpected.

The Black Dog

Every night, my bedtime, the black mongrel barks.
This dog is not a metaphor: it does not stand for
fury, depression, or (what everyone expects in poems)
Death. The neighbors leave it in their yard
behind our patio wall—a yard chockfull of lack,
without grass, a bush, or flowers. Magician Rain
performs one trick there: hardpack to mud.

This dog is not a happy dog, which is not
a projection: the dark beast, I mean, itself.
Its *ruff-ruffs* go on, on and on, until
the dog becomes hoarse. Then quiet
for just long enough you think it might stop.
This back-and-forth—barks, silence, barks—
is not unlike that cramped yard's reduced
repertoire: hardpack, or mud.

And I myself am torn between pity
and hatred: miserable dog, with rough,
monotone, sleep-annihilating bark.

Not a tragedy, then, affording its catharsis
of pity and fear, but a grinding ordinariness,
like habitual, nocturnal
grinding of teeth. And ineffectual
the would-be sleeper's curses, like

that shut-out mongrel's barking,
or how someone might feel (a merchant,
for example, an artist or inventor) after years
of work, failure, work, failure, work.

You want to know if I've spoken pleasantly
with the neighbors? They never answer
their door or let the black dog in. Bark.

Waking in Suburban AZ

5:00 a.m., with the dream
(a sweaty, real dream)
still speaking: "Let there be light."

Leave off scrounging, coyote,
in the green garbage bin, re-disappear
as dawn comes with your slouchy walk.

Pretty shell-full of liquid amber,
scorpion, back into your hole.

The humans are going to work.

Where did that rage come from? Am I being my mother?
How does a caterpillar melt down and alter?
What makes the universe expand, fast and faster?

—Asking about inside, about outside.

There is no god
to do our job.

Natural History Museum

—Mesa, Arizona

Today we saw the bones of a winged dinosaur, small raptor,
pictured it diving onto a meaty herbivore, ripping out chunks;

we saw a woolly mammoth skeleton from millions of years later
(O shaggy, tusked enormities our ancestors drove over cold cliffs!).

Also, a few Precambrian *Ediacara*—soft-bodied,
weird fauna from before the first mass extinction.

Five times, the earth has (mostly) stopped life to start over.

And what is the relation of what came after to what went before?

And, in a human life (short, yet so long to us), what is the relation?

—Each of us a planet on which life has (mostly) stopped to start over.
The same iron core, but above, the forms alter:

a small box made of jelly

a monster arthropod

a gargantuan herbivore, grazing in a stupor

a flying not-a-bird-yet, with teeth.

Desert Sunset Pavane

I walked alone with my friend,
I mean I walked with our long history—

real, unreal pink clouds,
as on a gilded baroque ceiling.

(Grandeur was never our tenor, but still. . . .)

There were the years of. . . .
And the years of. . . .
—So much of youth, a tender blunder.

Now, a wonder to converse,
un-vehement, nuanced.

Like children learning ballroom dancing
—careful of their posture,
remembering to smile,
proceeding with light gravity—
we step into old age.

Old Movies

Everyone knows the losses,
makes automatic, unconvincing noises
about what may be gained.

Wisdom, supposedly. A new ease
in one's thinning, wrinkled skin. Supposedly.

Sudden un-susceptibility to the (suddenly increased)
indifference of others.

A pleasantly dotty, enlarged scope of affection.

Maybe, in the final stretch, a colorful surge
of what-the-hell derring-do.

Supposedly.

　　Well, one thing I've noticed,
　　desert evenings, streaming Netflix:

old movies

　　　　　—when they came out, too overwhelmed
　　　　　by Cinemascope and pained envy
　　　　　of magnified, flawless faces—

　　now, I get.

Africa

Kenya, Namibia, Zambia, Somalia, Insomnia. . . .
You might think you're thinking, but you're not.

Proto-cogitation—like the single, low-watt "thought"
shared by the wildebeest herd stampeding, manifold,
to cross the river at some stupid, impossible spot.
Dozens slip off the cliff. (Too steep, mud-slick.)
Dozens quick-carcassed and crocodile-consumed.
The too-dumb-to-live still-living redirect
their half-thought and rush, jam-packed, back.

As Miss Stanwood (third grade) exclaimed: "Dunderheads!"

As Fulke Greville (1609) sighed: "O Wearisome condition of humanity!"

Somewhere are sensibly sleeping or clear-acting creatures.
The cheetah sprints to trip an impala. The leopard
had a bloody thought, now breakfast, stashed high in a tree.

D'où Venons Nous/ Que Sommes Nous/ Où Allons Nous

After black-painting these words (top-left corner),
Gauguin, convinced the rest of his life would be unsuccessful,
attempted suicide, unsuccessfully.

But that was Tahiti, 1897. It's 2013, blue digital 2:10
in suburban Arizona/Africa: hot sheets.

Under an acacia, bellies distended, the golden pride, heaped, sleeps.

Lands You'll Never See

On the Amazon, monkeys and red parrots
raucous in the canopy at dusk,
just outside our "tree-house" hotel room.

But it was canceled, our group trip to Brazil
(rumored kidnaps, political unrest):
and so, another place we'll never go.

No barely bathing-suited *Cariocas*
screen-testing for dreams at Ipanema.
No sugarcane *cachaça* to make us dizzy

—"the little blond," they call it, spitting out
the first gold mouthful for a patron saint.
Not to see this, never to do that,

the way you'll never, say, become an athlete
or an architect or astronaut—
or any of us in this life be free

of handed-down, hobbling unself-ease,
given the supply of hobbled parents,
no doubt just as hobbled in Brazil.

Gilded baroque chocolate-box churches;
scores of exotic fruit drinks in Manaus
(river-port old slave town with its lean-tos,

brown-water rot and crumbling opera house);
soapstone statues of prophets in Ouro Prêto
sculpted by the leprous "Little Cripple"

who worked with special tools strapped to his wrists.
City-nesting vultures and slaughtered forests;
abraços, toxic beaches, grilled meat, drums.

One of several lands you'll never see,
like the Sahara: young Wodaabe men
lined up for the annual beauty contest

(darkened lips and shock-white, kohl-rimmed eyes),
each vying to be chosen by girl judges,
maybe for marriage, maybe for one night.

Carnival, *cafezinhos,* caravans
—burdened camels so balanced over the sand
their two-toed hooves leave no prints where they pass.

Palm Wrong Song

Windmill Palm, Monkey Tail, Bottle Palm, Scrub Palm, Silver Saw Palmetto. . . .
Beyond the distinction between palmate and pinnate, there's this array,

like the bewildering number of ways we can go wrong:
Snake Fruit Palm, Mosquito Palm, Brittle Thatch, Black Wanga.

There exist some 2600 species, including different-colored wrongs
(Red Lemur, Purple Yatay, Orange Collar, Silver Joey),

as well as low-life, rowdy wrongs
(Red Neck Palm, Cuban Belly, Vicious Hairy Mary),

and grand dynastic wrongs, a little mad from incestuous in-breeding
(Andean Royal Palm, Myola King Palm, Nicobar Majestic)—

which reminds me of wrongs to populate a Faulkner county:
Major Jenkins, Slender Lady, Stumpy Palm, Mute.

The family *Palmae,* like Ancient Wrong, dates from the late Cretaceous.

Nubian Desert Palm, Puerto Rican Hat, Canary Island Date:
no matter where I go, a gift for wrong attends me.

Can you forgive me, ever, for my *Black Basselinia?*
Will you love me in spite of my *Hedgehog Rattan?*

(You can't count my sullen *Sago* because it's really a cycad.)

Giant Window Palm, Brain Seed Palm, Walking Stick Palm:
is there a way out, if we think it through, before it's too late?

I promise never again to bring up your *Brazilian Needle.*
Someday we'll share a laugh over *West African Wine Palm.*

Have I told you, *Zebra Fishtail, Tibetan Sugar Palm, Blue Hesper,*
have I mentioned, *Chiqui-chiqui,* how sweet you are, and rare?

Cup

What could be better

    (in a life wanting

a father, something better

    than the ghost of a father)

than these in-process rooms, so much better

    than our last, crumbling house,

in this new state where we're happier, better—

    she (whose bitter mother

beat her, could do no better)

    in the study with her orange

mug of coffee, black, sugared, but not better

    than my own green mug of café au lait,

working, both, to make better

stanzas, rooms, lives.

And you, toiling to make it better,

whatever your it is. Each has a cup.

The Art of Living

We have more than a room—rooms!—in our little house.

All over America people are getting fat in front of their flat-screens, eating junk.

All over our pretty house, yesterday, grievance plastered the walls.

I'm just sayin'.

Perpetrating misery in (practically) luxury's lap; how evil is that?

It's so last week, so over.

Get up, little darlin'. I'll make you an egg.

New Year

Praise to the man or woman who stays open
to the river of each day. Praise
to her or him who keeps, past sixty
and in all weathers, an open heart.

Remember nineteen? The pair of us walking at midnight
in the city and stopping at someone's, anyone's, front stairs
(those concrete steps, the Richmond in San Francisco)
—ignoring the cold, ignoring the strangers who must
be annoyed inside—to sit and talk excitedly, laughing
or moving ourselves to tears like Chekhov's drunken Russians,
needing to *say* the vast, inrushing perceptions of just one day.

You weren't the one I walked with. I let the poem lie,
knowing it wouldn't matter: you'd have your own city,
you'd have been giddy before you grew old, and apprised.

Praise to the man or woman who stays open
to the river of each day. Praise
to her or him who keeps, past sixty
and in all weathers, an open heart.

IV

Beauty

—*After reading Lucy Grealy's* Autobiography of a Face

In this unbeautiful place,
my experiment-in-living summer sublet

with its cheap, unstained bookcases
and mismatched kitchen chairs with stains,

I wonder about beauty, worrying
that old-bone question like a dog.

And I woo her, Beauty.

With the salt lick of open books,
with the clear pond of music.

It's important that I am alone,
like someone under kidnappers' instructions,
compelled to meet in darkness and pay ransom.

Important to think with care of those I love.
Important carefully, gently, to forget them,

since the habit of tenderness attracts her,
since she wants you waiting just for her.

Her demands are contradictory, crazy:
formal attentions and familiar ease,
bestirring purpose and vacant lassitude,
a passion for order and disordered passion.

One day, she'll meet you only *en plein air*
(yes, she likes French champagne—and beer);
the next, it's got to be your stuffy room.

At whim, she'll take up with *anyone!*

Why bother, then, with difficult Beauty?

    * * *

Here's a true story about suffering and Beauty:

the child was disfigured badly
by an operation at age nine
for cancer of the jaw.

After two years of radiation
and weekly, sickening chemo,
she went back to school.

When away from that ordeal
—the cafeteria, the jeering boys—
she worked in a stable

grooming and feeding horses,
touching their soft bellies,
listening to their stomachs

and smelling their breath.
When, in pain, she couldn't sleep
she'd get up and call; she'd let

the phone ring in the barn.

The Resistant Reader in the Age of Memoir

In her book, she said the guiding principle
was guarding against irreparable losses;
she'd managed to live so as

to avoid any major cause of regret.

Anyone who's done that, raise your hand:
you're excused from this poem.

As for us who remain, let's go around
the circle and list our regrets.
For the stuporous, self-evading hours.

For off-hand, wounding sarcasms.

For narcissistic hatred of the imperfect
body, which has hampered love.

For fatigued, five o'clock snapping
at the over-amped three-year-old.
For withholding, out of harbored

resentment, the wholehearted response.

For everyday, ape-in-hierarchy,
lies of assent. . . .

But maybe she meant larger,
one-time-only things avoided?
The sale of the family house, say,

an abortion, the laceration of divorce?

But what servility was kept with that house,
what cowardice clung to with the brave

delivery of the baby, what fear of darkness
retained with the long-lasting marriage?
(And is there a word for the regret

of having too few regrets?

There must be. In French?)
Remember that adolescent moment, poised

before first sex—with already,
how many regrets? Who knows the number
of planets where life might start over?

On one, an ocean with a new tide. Trees, maybe?

So beautiful. They grow and fall in one place,
never experiencing irreparable loss.

Still

—Watching on YouTube the great ballerina Margot Fonteyn

What will we not do
to avoid it, this opposite
of distraction,

this centered attention?
But, now, here it is—
what we'd almost forgotten to want.

    In *The Sleeping Beauty,*
    Fonteyn's Rose Adagio:

    sur la pointe
    she balances

    —long seconds, impossible!—

    beside each of four suitors
    before extending her arm to take
                   his
                     his
                       his
                         his

hand,

so that one by one
each now-tethered partner
can walk, princely, around her

—presenting—

while, on point, in *attitude,*

she turns
slowly, cleanly
before us
and for us
being

still somehow still.

Untitled

—Mark Rothko, Untitled, *1954*

This is where I want to live.
Is it evening, is it morning? I don't know.

What a mango light, rising from soft stripes
of butter and tomato above a block of plum.

But there's no earthly food here, no need
for other food than stripes and blocks and hue.

At the base—recalling Brueghel's scrawny
bushes in the foreground of *Hunters in the Snow*—

a blurred red-orange feathers upward
into plum. But thinly the fresh mango sidles down

to border all, the way the cosmos is and holds
the stars of which we are a part—though squalid

we are, sometimes, as stars can never be,
nor this man's art. It's cool

out there (and here), unutterably cold,
but also warm, and home.

Maker's Mark

Because I had nothing to say I did the wash.

I could have gone to a matinee.
I could have gone to see the manatee
at the zoo to avoid monotony.

I could have gone to the mall.

I did the wash.

And while the light things were washing
I ate thick-sliced tomato on sourdough with salt.

And while the light things were drying
and the dark things were washing
I read a chapter in *The Secret Life of Dust*.

And while the dark things were drying
and the orange towels were washing
I lay down and listened to an old CD.

And when the perilous towels that bleed
were finally in the dryer
I poured a *demi-tasse* of Maker's Mark.

By that time the setting sun
through the two west-facing windows
(one bare, one with Venetian blinds)
was making a pair of paintings on the wall:

      a Rothko
      rectangle
      of rose
floating on a mysterious dark band
      above a block
      of palest
      corn-silk gold.

Beside it hung an almost colorless grid
with hand-drawn equidistant horizontal
nearly invisible lines: an Agnes Martin!

It could have been pouring rain.
I could have been poor again
or gored by pain

as somebody out there was.

Someone else was going from a boardroom
to a barroom
attempting to ward off boredom.

But I sat at this exclusive,
historic opening: Great American
Paintings That Can Change!

Later, darkness made her drawn-out entrance
and a crescent moon ascended.

None of us had anything to say.

Foreign Film Series

—With Diane

In Paris or at bourgeois seaside resorts,
walking or sitting at cafés or sprawled on grass,

in bathing suits or sweaters, how they can talk!
—the men, the women, even little girls,

holding forth about what they want from love.
What do I want from love? Just what I've got,

and I don't feel like telling what that is!
When fireflies arrive in the still yard,

I watch the bushes noiseless with surprises.
When pain calls late at night and wakes me up,

pain and I conduct our chat in silence.
When, after thirty years, I'm riveted

by gray eyes and a voice proposing how
a woman's shifting posture on a sofa

discloses what her practiced, self-protective
conversation tries to hide, and how

Rohmer, in all his scenes, has sympathy
for anyone who tries to civilize

brutish, unpredictable desire
with hapless plans, with speeches or reticence,

I have about as much breath left for talking
as does a traveler on the coastal highway,

someone who for too long has lived inland,
rounding a curve and sighting the first wave.

The Farnsworth House

—The Glass House, Mies van der Rohe, 1951

Magic mixes opposites,
mixes categories.

Arcimboldi's faces
made of vegetables;
the brown-breasted, blue-backed bird
that juxtaposes earth and air;
or, my friend adds, the lioness
that is "sunlight on four feet."

And this all-window house:

outside turns into inside,
what protects exposes,
rigidity reduplicates
the surrounding trees' flux.

(Now view the patio: thick-slabbed travertine

can float.)

Wide panes and white-painted
steel at right angles—

insertion asserting
with precision and proportion:
what you thought unnatural
is nature.

To John Clare

—"snug as comfort's wishes ever lay"

So, John, the summer's come again—
the great variety of birds is gone,
meadowland is scarce to dream upon,

and our many poets seldom rhyme.
Keats, who shared your publisher, has fame
for his late odes. You're best known for "I am—

yet what I am, none cares or knows," written
when you were old, in the asylum. Freshmen
in college recite your anguish with conviction:

in the anthology, you speak for *them*.
A deep pink English rose now bears your name.
None of us knows, do we, what we'll become?

You became like your badger by the end—
thickset and burrowing and shy of men;
wounded and mad, you thought you were Lord Byron.

You were your losses' keeper. Enclosured freedom.
You were loafing's laborer. The sum
of subtractions: Mary, the fields, hope of acclaim.

You gave in to ale, but stuck to rustic diction:
your *totter* grass and *baulks* between the grain,
your *whewing* larks and *drowking* flowers at noon

and *sturting* hares. Editors preserve them
now, let stand what's been cut down. The elm
trees, their soft *suthering.* You, John—"homeless at home."

Easy Street Sonnet

—Late June, Ohio

On the front porch, early in vacation
on our still-preserved Victorian
red-brick street, looking through
one side, east, at the view
of successive porches—cream
railings, brick steps, and gray-green
slate roofs. A study in perspective—a kind
of hall of diminishing porches, or a kind

of train made up of boxcar-porches, one
after another into the distance. And just when
I thought that, a train went by and I heard
the wheel-clack and then some bird
—completing the new setup without a hassle—
stood in for an old-fashioned engine whistle!

Lear's Macaw *(Anodorhynchus leari)*

A nineteenth-century profile
illustration of a Brazilian
zoo-captive in Britain,
"sleepy-eyed" (from age
or poor nutrition):
blue-suede-footed, claw

over branch above
the block-print label,
Macrocercus hyacinthinus,
the Hyacinthine Macaw,
which it was not.
Napoleon's nephew spotted

the distinction and named
the species, based on Lear's
depiction, and on a single
skin kept in the Paris
Musée d'Histoire Naturelle;
but where and how

the bird lived in the wild
tantalized discovery for
more than a century
until, in dry northeast
Brazil, Dr. Helmut Sick,
decades deep in searching,

finally found (late
December, 1978) cadmium
in cadmium, in flight!
These yellow-eye-ringed,
long-winged, thirty-inch
stunt pilots only nest

in sandstone cliffs which
echo their harsh cries
each dusk, and feed
on nuts of the licuri palm—
the rarest of the wild macaws,
supposedly "protected,"

but still vanishing, still poached.
(The poor sell cheap to dealers
who deliver to the rich
the speaking sky: a sheik
with his menagerie; a Yorkshire
breeder; a secret trader,

Swiss.) The Highgate teenager
who drew the bird for needed
money and for his *Family
of the Psittacidae* was
lonely, playful, large-
beaked, queer, and rare.

Beethoven's *Pastoral*

Yellow
But nothing sour

A world without
A beating to walk into

And after the Fifth
Made by himself

Not himself
Jocund

Daffodils, wind-bent
But no blows

Taking It Slow

—For George Harrison (1943-2001)

The trees don't mind,
and their whispering is companionable.

The world of people minds
when you are old, ill perhaps, a little dim

from pain—even though you're
good-willed and willing,

knowledgeable, even, about some things,
but tired. The world of people is afraid.

But you, small-handed red maple,
and you, Noh-ghost paper birch,

you don't mind—do you?—if I sit
in the slight breeze and listen

to your song of *years-go-by,*
flicker-patter, it's-all-right.

Here she comes, taking her own
sweet time going, the sun.

Late Harvest

—After Rilke's "Herbsttag"

Time, it is time.
Summer has been
long-stretched-out, full.
Go ahead, Fall:
shrink down the days
and sugar the grapes
for late-harvest wine.

Anyone still unknown
to herself will stay,
probably, that way.
Anyone unlinked by love
will be love-
left-out now—waking,
mind-pacing
up and down
up and down,
restless as leaf-bits
and papers in the street.

Notes

p. 5: The phrase "Dancing in the dark" is from the popular song of that title, music by Arthur Schwartz, lyrics by Howard Dietz (1931); "Death's second self" is from Shakespeare's Sonnet 73, where it is used in reference to night.

p. 39: The quotation is from Fulke Greville's *The Tragedy of Mustapha* (1609).

pp. 51–52: As a child, Lucy Grealy was treated for Ewing's sarcoma (a malignant tumor of the bone or soft tissue) in her jaw. Surgery left her facially deformed, and she underwent, in youth and then adulthood, more than thirty painful and never fully successful reconstructive operations. She died in 2002, at the age of thirty-nine. The second section borrows some phrasing from Lucy Grealy's memoir, *Autobiography of a Face.*

p. 66: The epigraph is from one of Clare's many poems about birds, "The Yellow Wagtail's Nest." "Homeless at home," in the final line, is a quotation from Clare's brief *Journey out of Essex,* which records his arduous three-day walk in July 1841 from the High Beach Asylum to his home in Northborough. Clare's first, lost love was Mary Joyce.

p. 71: It is commonly thought that Beethoven's early years included the violence of frequent beatings. Most contemporary reports come from Gottfried and Cäcilia Fischer, whose father owned the house where the Beethovens lived when Ludwig was a child: *Des Bonner Bäckmeisters Gottfried Fischer: Aufzeichnungen über Beethovens Jugend,* ed. Joseph Schmidt-Görg (Bonne Beethovenhaus, 1971). Or, see Maynard Solomon's biography *Beethoven* (New York: Schirmer Books, 1998), pp. 23–24.

Jeredith Merrin—brought up in the Pacific Northwest—took her M.A. in English (specializing in Chaucer), followed by a Ph.D. from U.C. Berkeley in Anglo-American Poetry and Poetics. *Cup,* a special honoree in the 2013 Able Muse Book Award, is her third collection; her previous books, *Shift* and *Bat Ode,* appeared in the University of Chicago Press Phoenix Poets series. She's authored an influential book of criticism on Marianne Moore and Elizabeth Bishop, and her reviews and essays (on Moore, Bishop, Clare, Mew, Amichai, and others) have appeared in *The Southern Review* and elsewhere. Her poems may be found in such journals as *Paris Review, Slate, Ploughshares, Southwest Review,* and *Yale Review.* A retired Professor of English (The Ohio State University), she lives near Phoenix.

ALSO FROM ABLE MUSE PRESS

William Baer, *Times Square and Other Stories*

Melissa Balmain, *Walking in on People – Poems*

Ben Berman, *Strange Borderlands – Poems*

Michael Cantor, *Life in the Second Circle – Poems*

Catherine Chandler, *Lines of Flight – Poems*

William Conelly, *Uncontested Grounds – Poems*

Maryann Corbett, *Credo for the Checkout Line in Winter – Poems*

John Drury, *Sea Level Rising – Poems*

D.R. Goodman, *Greed: A Confession – Poems*

Margaret Ann Griffiths, *Grasshopper – The Poetry of M A Griffiths*

Ellen Kaufman, *House Music – Poems*

Carol Light, *Heaven from Steam – Poems*

April Lindner, *This Bed Our Bodies Shaped – Poems*

Martin McGovern, *Bad Fame – Poems*

Richard Newman, *All the Wasted Beauty of the World – Poems*

Frank Osen, *Virtue, Big as Sin – Poems*

Alexander Pepple (Editor), *Able Muse Anthology*

Alexander Pepple (Editor), *Able Muse – a review of poetry, prose & art*
  (semiannual issues, Winter 2010 onward)

James Pollock, *Sailing to Babylon – Poems*

Aaron Poochigian, *The Cosmic Purr – Poems*

Stephen Scaer, *Pumpkin Chucking – Poems*

Hollis Seamon, *Corporeality – Stories*

Matthew Buckley Smith, *Dirge for an Imaginary World – Poems*

Barbara Ellen Sorensen, *Compositions of the Dead Playing Flutes – Poems*

Wendy Videlock, *The Dark Gnu and Other Poems*

Wendy Videlock, *Nevertheless – Poems*

Wendy Videlock, *Slingshots and Love Plums – Poems*

Richard Wakefield, *A Vertical Mile – Poems*

Chelsea Woodard, *Vellum – Poems*

www.ablemusepress.com

www.ingramcontent.com/pod-product-compliance
Lightning Source LLC
Chambersburg PA
CBHW022014080426
42733CB00007B/594